Pebble®

My World

States
in My World

by Ella Cane

Consulting Editor: Gail Saunders-Smith, PhD

CAPSTONE PRESS
a capstone imprint

Pebble Books are published by Capstone Press,
1710 Roe Crest Drive, North Mankato, Minnesota 56003
www.capstonepub.com

Library of Congress Cataloging-in-Publication Data
Cane, Ella.
States in my world / by Ella Cane.
pages cm. — (Pebble books. My world)
Includes index.
ISBN 978-1-4765-3121-2 (library binding)
ISBN 978-1-4765-3463-3 (paperback)
ISBN 978-1-4765-3469-5 (ebook pdf)
1. United States—Juvenile literature. I. Title.
E180.C36 2014
973—dc23   2013005895

Summary: Simple text and full-color photographs introduce states to the reader.

Note to Parents and Teachers
The My World set supports national curriculum standards
for social studies related to people, places, and environments.
This book describes and illustrates states. The images support
early readers in understanding the text. The repetition of words
and phrases helps early readers learn new words. This book
also introduces early readers to subject-specific vocabulary
words, which are defined in the Glossary section. Early readers
may need assistance to read some words and to use the Table
of Contents, Glossary, Read More, Internet Sites, and Index
sections of the book.

Printed in the United States   5717

Table of Contents

What Is a State? 5

People and Government 9

Landforms 15

Biggest and Smallest 19

Glossary 22

Read More 23

Internet Sites 23

Index 24

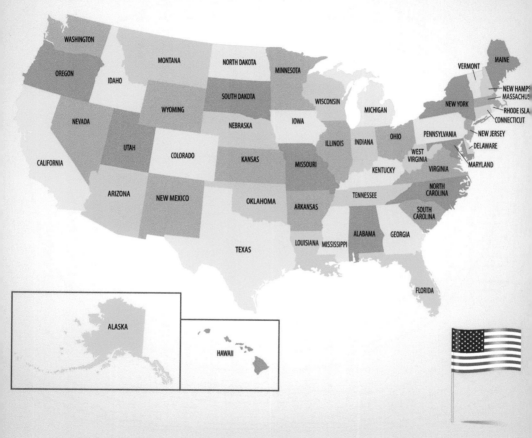

WASHINGTON
MONTANA
NORTH DAKOTA
MINNESOTA
VERMONT
MAINE
OREGON
IDAHO
SOUTH DAKOTA
WISCONSIN
NEW HAMPS
NEW YORK
MASSACHUS
WYOMING
NEBRASKA
IOWA
MICHIGAN
RHODE ISLA
NEVADA
CONNECTICUT
ILLINOIS
INDIANA
OHIO
PENNSYLVANIA
NEW JERSEY
UTAH
COLORADO
KANSAS
MISSOURI
WEST
VIRGINIA
DELAWARE
CALIFORNIA
KENTUCKY
VIRGINIA
MARYLAND
ARIZONA
NEW MEXICO
OKLAHOMA
ARKANSAS
TENNESSEE
NORTH
CAROLINA
SOUTH
CAROLINA
ALABAMA
GEORGIA
TEXAS
LOUISIANA
MISSISSIPPI
FLORIDA

ALASKA

HAWAII

What Is a State?

The United States
has 50 states.
Each state has
many cities and towns.

A state is an organized community. It's part of a larger government.

Wyoming

People and Government

California has the most people of any state. The fewest people live in Wyoming.

The people of each state
elect leaders.
The top leader of a state
is called a governor.

Each state also has
representatives and senators.
They are elected to serve
in the U.S. Congress.

Landforms

A state's landforms depend on its location. The Rocky Mountains stretch from Montana to New Mexico.

The Great Plains sweep across North Dakota to Texas.

RHODE ISL...

DELAWARE

TEXAS

ALASKA

Biggest and Smallest

The largest states in size are Alaska and Texas. Delaware and Rhode Island are the smallest states.

Each state in the
United States is different.
What do you know
about your state?

Glossary

community—a group of people who live in the same area

Congress—the elected group of people who make laws for the United States

government—the group of people who make laws, rules, and decisions for a country or state

governor—a person elected to be the head of a state's government

landform—a natural feature of the land

plain—a large, flat area of land with few trees

representative—a person elected to serve the U.S. government in Congress; a representative serves in the House

senator—a person elected to serve the U.S. government in Congress; a senator serves in the Senate

Read More

Rose, Hayley. *Fifo 50 States.* Scottsdale, Ariz.: Inkwell Productions, 2007.

Schuh, Mari. *The U.S. House of Representatives.* The U.S. Government. Mankato, Minn.: Capstone Press, 2011.

Wooster, Patricia. *Show Me the United States: My First Picture Encyclopedia.* My First Picture Encyclopedias. North Mankato, Minn.: Capstone Press, 2013.

Internet Sites

FactHound offers a safe, fun way to find Internet sites related to this book. All of the sites on FactHound have been researched by our staff.

Here's all you do:

Visit *www.facthound.com*

Type in this code: 9781476531212

Check out projects, games and lots more at
www.capstonekids.com

Index

Alaska, 19
California, 9
communities, 7
Congress, 13
Delaware, 19
electing leaders, 11, 13
governments, 7
governors, 11
Great Plains, 17
landforms, 15

Montana, 15
New Mexico, 15
North Dakota, 17
representatives, 13
Rhode Island, 19
Rocky Mountains, 15
senators, 13
Texas, 17, 19
Wyoming, 9

Word Count: 129
Grade: 1
Early-Intervention Level: 18

Editorial Credits
Shelly Lyons, editor; Juliette Peters, designer; Marcie Spence, media researcher;
Eric Manske, production specialist

Photo Credits
Capstone Studio: Karon Dubke, 20; Corbis: Bettmann, 12; Getty Images: R. Darren
Price/The State/MCT, 10; Shutterstock: Alex and Anna, 4, 18, dalmingo, cover
(front), Francesco Dazzi, 6, Jacek Fulawka, cover (background), Jerry Sanchez, 8,
Lorcel, 1, Peter Kunasz, 14, Tyler Olson, 16